HMH | (into) **Reading**™

my Book 4

Authors and Advisors

Alma Flor Ada • Kylene Beers • F. Isabel Campoy

Joyce Armstrong Carroll • Nathan Clemens

Anne Cunningham • Martha C. Hougen

Elena Izquierdo • Carol Jago • Erik Palmer

Robert E. Probst • Shane Templeton • Julie Washington

Contributing Consultants

David Dockterman • Mindset Works®

Jill Eggleton

Printed in the U.S.A.

ISBN   978-1-328-51692-3

10   0868   27 26 25 24 23 22

4500845437   C D E F G

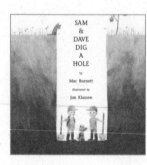

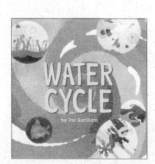

MODULE 8

Tell Me a Story

6

The Big Outdoors

"Drops that gather one by one
finally become a sea."

—Persian Proverb

How do things in nature change?

Get Curious Video

Words About the Natural World

Complete the Vocabulary Network to show what you
know about the words.

cycle
Meaning: A **cycle** is a group of events that repeat in the same order.

Synonyms and Antonyms	Drawing

liquid

Meaning: A **liquid** is something that you can pour, like water or milk.

Synonyms and Antonyms	Drawing

evaporation

Meaning: **Evaporation** is when a liquid turns into a gas.

Synonyms and Antonyms	Drawing

Short Read

READ Together

STORM REPORT

The clouds get dark.
The wind blows.
FLASH! BOOM!
It's a storm!

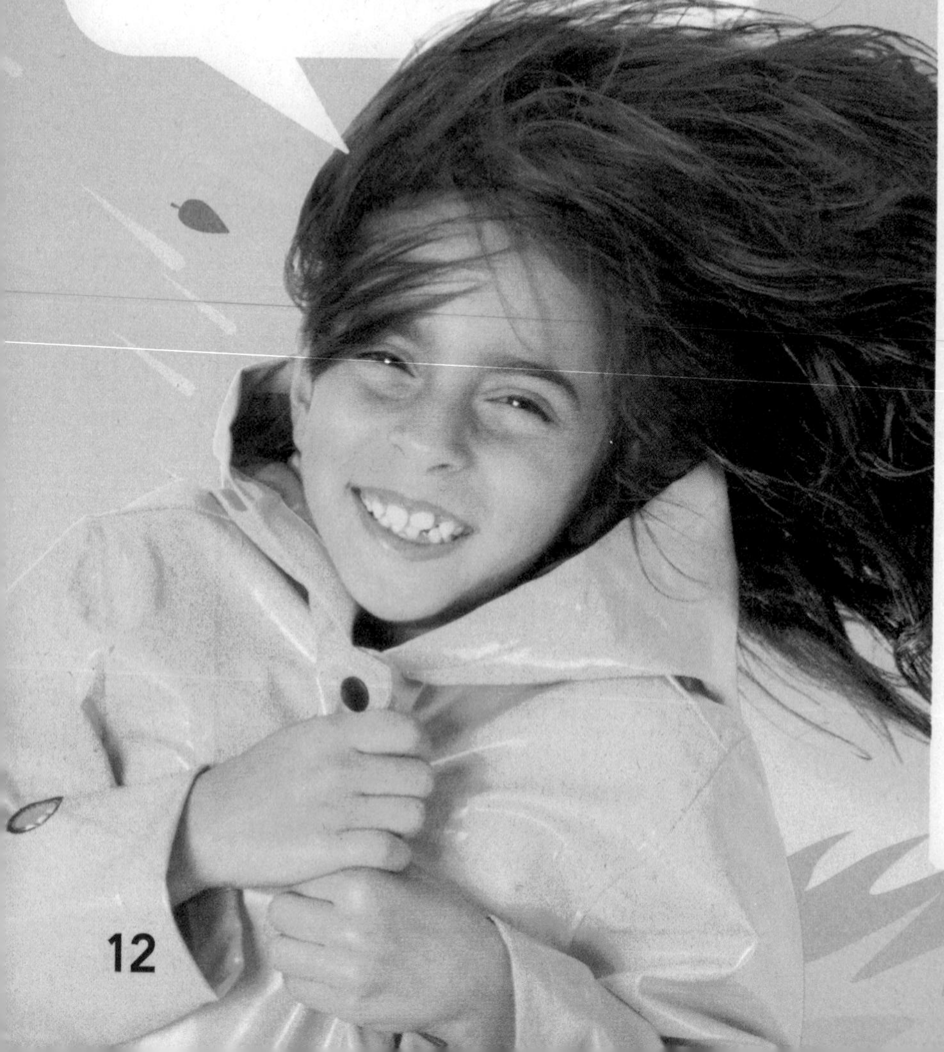

Do you want to find out about storms? Then read a great book called Big Storms. It is about all kinds of powerful storms. Big snowstorms are called blizzards. There are even big dust storms!

You will see exciting photos of real storms. One picture shows a huge bolt of lightning. Another one shows a blizzard. The snow is up to the windows of the houses!

blizzard

dust storm

thunderstorm

hurricane

tornado

Another reason to read this book is to find out how to stay safe in storms. I learned a good tip. When thunder roars, go indoors! Big Storms is such an interesting book. Read it soon!

Prepare to Read

GENRE STUDY **Fantasy** stories have made-up events that could not really happen. Look for:

- make-believe parts of the setting and events
- problems and resolutions
- ways pictures and words help you understand the story

SET A PURPOSE Read to make smart guesses, or **inferences**, about things the author does not say. Use what you know and clues in the story.

POWER WORDS
mission
spectacular
break
problem
direction
landed

Meet Jon Klassen.

SAM
&
DAVE
DIG
A
HOLE

by

Mac Barnett

illustrated by

Jon Klassen

On Monday Sam and Dave dug a hole.

"When should we stop digging?" asked Sam.
"We are on a mission," said Dave.
"We won't stop digging until we find
something spectacular."

The hole got so deep that their heads were underground.
But they still had not found anything spectacular.
"We need to keep digging," said Dave.

So they kept digging.

They took a break.
Dave drank chocolate milk
out of a canteen.
Sam ate animal cookies he had wrapped
in their grandfather's kerchief.
"Maybe," said Dave,
"the problem is that we are
digging straight down."
"Yes," said Sam.
"That could be the problem."
"I think we should dig in
another direction," said Dave.
"Yes," said Sam.
"That is a good idea."

"I have a new idea," said Dave.
"Let's split up."
"Really?" said Sam.
"Just for a little while," said Dave.
"It will help our chances."

So Dave went one way,

and Sam went another.

But they did not find
anything spectacular.
"Maybe we should go back
to digging straight down,"
said Dave.
"Yes," said Sam.
"That is a good idea."

Sam and Dave ran out of chocolate milk.
But they kept digging.
They shared the last animal cookie.
But they kept digging.

After a while Sam sat down.
"Dave," he said, "I am tired.
I cannot dig anymore."
"I am tired too," said Dave.
"We should take a rest."
Sam and Dave fell asleep.

Then Sam and Dave were falling.

Sam and Dave fell down,

down,

down,

until they landed in the soft dirt.

"Well," said Sam.
"Well," said Dave.
"That was pretty spectacular."

And they went inside
for chocolate milk and animal cookies.

Use details from **Sam & Dave Dig a Hole** to answer these questions with a partner.

1. **Make Inferences** How can you tell that the boys are good friends?

2. What makes the boys' adventure spectacular?

Talking Tip

Take turns talking. When it is your turn, add on to your partner's idea.

My idea is _____.

Write a Message

PROMPT Think of a part of the story when
Sam and Dave almost find something spectacular.
What message could you send to them to help
them find it?

PLAN Draw a map. Show where Sam and Dave
are and how to get to the spectacular thing.

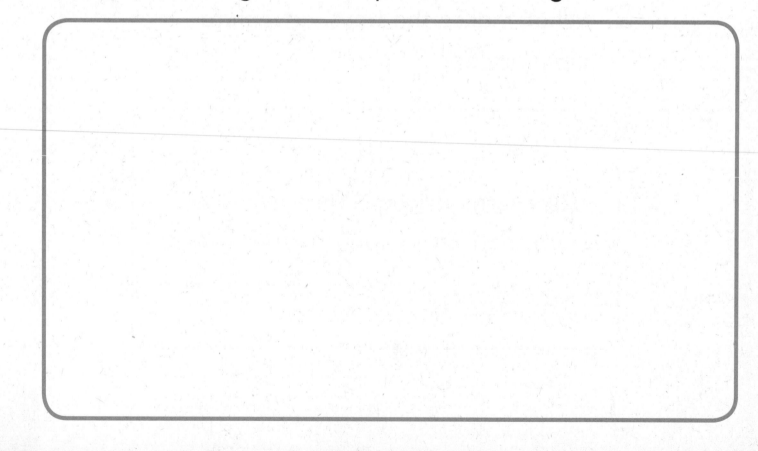

WRITE Now write a message to Sam and Dave. Tell them how to find the spectacular thing. Remember to:

- Use a capital letter to begin each sentence and to write the word **I**.

- Use words to tell which way to go, like **left, right, up, down, above,** and **below**.

_____

- -

_____

- -

_____

- -

_____

- -

_____

Prepare to Read

GENRE STUDY **Fantasy** stories have made-up events that could not really happen.

MAKE A PREDICTION Preview **Ron and Tron**. Ron and Tron live on different planets. Think about how fantasy stories have make-believe events. What do you think will happen?

_____

- -

_____

- -

_____

SET A PURPOSE Read to find out what Ron and Tron do and to see if your prediction is right. If not, think about what a fantasy story is like and make a new prediction.

Ron and Tron

READ Does a narrator outside the story or a character in the story tell the very beginning? How do you know? Who writes the letter? Underline words that help you know who is telling this part of the story.

Ron and Tron live far away from each other. They write to keep in touch.

Hi Tron,
  Last week, I was digging deep under the sea on my planet. I found red and green gems! They glow and sparkle. You like to dig for gems too, so come visit me!
            Your friend,
            Ron ▶

Close Reading Tip

Is your prediction right so far? If not, think about the genre and make a new prediction.

33

READ Who tells the part of the story at the top of the page? <u>Underline</u> words that help you know. Does a character in the story or a narrator outside the story tell the end? How do you know?

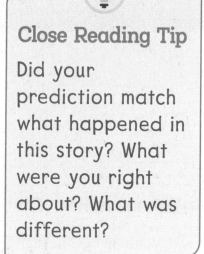

Close Reading Tip

Did your prediction match what happened in this story? What were you right about? What was different?

Hi Ron!

   You are right! I DO like to dig and explore. But do you want to come visit me first? We can help each other look for gems in the deep, dark caves on my planet.

                      Your pal,

                      Tron

Ron went to Tron's planet. They looked in the caves. No gems! But they found lots of bats and had a good time anyway.

CHECK MY UNDERSTANDING

Ron and Tron found bats because

_____

- - - - - - - - - - - - - - - - - -

_____

- - - - - - - - - - - - - - - - - -

_____

WRITE ABOUT IT How can you tell that Ron and Tron are friends? Write sentences. Use details from the story to explain why.

Prepare to Read

GENRE STUDY **Informational text** is nonfiction. It gives facts about a topic. Look for:

- facts about the world

- photos with labels

- ways pictures and words help you understand the text

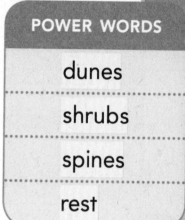

POWER WORDS

dunes

shrubs

spines

rest

SET A PURPOSE As you read, stop and think if you don't understand something. Reread, look at the pictures, use what you already know, or ask yourself questions.

Build Background: Water Matters!

Deserts

by Quinn M. Arnold

Hello, desert!

Hot deserts are dry. They do not get much rain.

The biggest hot
desert is the Sahara.

Deserts may be rocky or sandy. Sometimes they have rocks and sand.

Sandy deserts may
have tall dunes.
Snakes slide over
the sand.

Plants and animals
adapt to the desert.
Animals get water
from food they eat.

Shrubs and wildflowers
have long roots. They can
reach water far below.

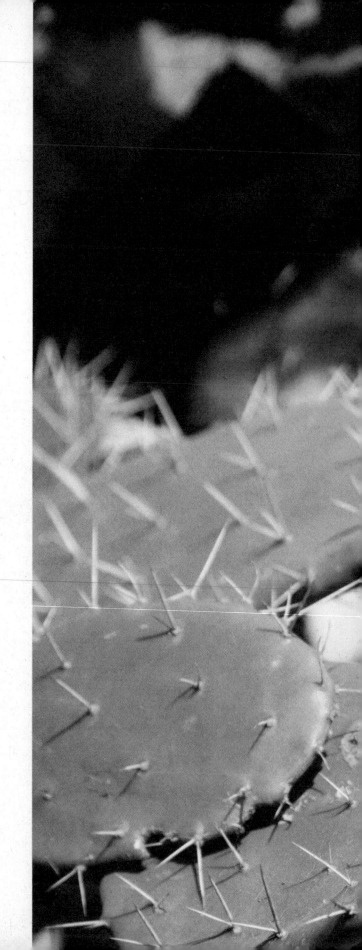

Some cacti grow
more than 40
feet tall. They
store water.

Sharp spines
keep many
animals away.

The hot desert sun warms lizards.

Jackrabbits rest in shade.
Foxes come out of their
dens at night.

47

Picture a Desert

dune

palm tree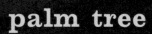

scorpion

sand

48

Sonoran Desert

cactus

rocks

spine

gopher snake

wildflowers

49

Goodbye,
desert!

Deserts

Use details from **Deserts** to answer these questions with a partner.

1. **Monitor and Clarify** When you came to a part you did not understand, what did you do to figure it out?

2. How do animals get food, water, and shelter in a desert?

Listening Tip

Listen carefully. Think about what your partner is saying and what you learn.

Write a Description

PROMPT How can you describe the land or a living thing from **Deserts** for someone who has never seen it? Use details from the words and photos to explain.

PLAN First, write your topic. Then write words and draw pictures to describe it.

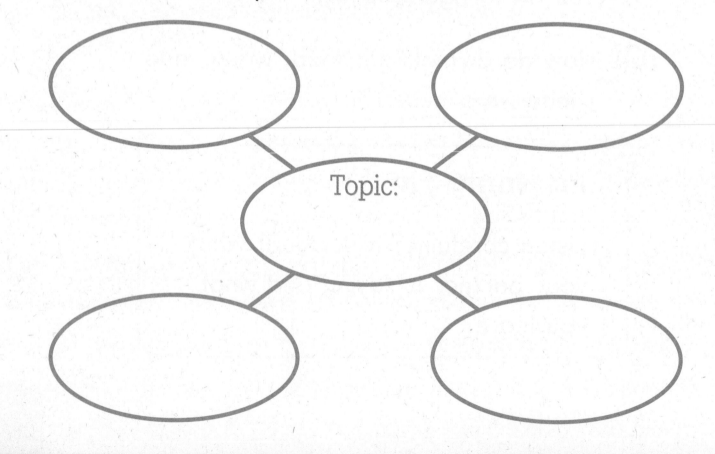

Topic:

WRITE Now write sentences to describe the desert land or desert creature. Remember to:

Deserts
by Quinn M. Arnold

- Be sure each sentence tells about your topic.

- Use words to describe colors, sizes, how things feel, and other details.

Prepare to Read

GENRE STUDY **Informational text** is nonfiction. It gives facts about a topic.

MAKE A PREDICTION Preview **How an Island Is Made**. First, there is a volcano. Then, there is an island! What do you think you will learn?

_____

- -

_____

- -

_____

- -

_____

SET A PURPOSE Read to find out one way that islands are made. Find out if your prediction is right. If not, make a new prediction as you read.

How an Island Is Made

READ What happens to the lava from the volcano?

Islands have water all around them. How is an island made? One way is from a volcano on the bottom of the sea. Hot lava rises up out of the volcano. The water makes the lava cold. This turns it into rock. ▶

Close Reading Tip

Circle words you don't know. Then figure them out.

CHECK MY UNDERSTANDING

What could you do to help yourself if you didn't understand this part of the text?

_____

- - - - - - - - - - - - - - - - - - -

_____

- - - - - - - - - - - - - - - - - - -

_____

READ <u>Underline</u> important things that happen after the lava comes out.

More and more lava comes out of the volcano. The pile of rock gets bigger. It gets so big that it comes up out of the water. A new island is made!

After a long time, plants will grow on the land. Birds and other animals will live here, too. Their home will be this island that was once just a volcano on the bottom of the sea.

CHECK MY UNDERSTANDING

What main thing, or central idea, is this text about?

_____

--- --- --- --- --- --- --- --- --- ---

_____

_____

--- --- --- --- --- --- --- --- --- ---

_____

_____

--- --- --- --- --- --- --- --- --- ---

_____

56

WRITE ABOUT IT Write a story to tell your classmates about a day you spend on the new island. What is it like? Use describing words. Draw it on another sheet of paper.

_____

- -

_____

_____

- -

_____

_____

- -

_____

_____

- -

_____

_____

- -

_____

_____

- -

_____

Prepare to Read

GENRE STUDY **Procedural texts** tell how to do or make something. Look for:

- directions to follow

- steps that show order

- pictures that show what the final project will look like

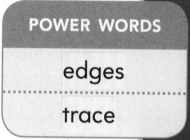

POWER WORDS

edges

trace

SET A PURPOSE Read to understand the most important ideas. Look for details in the words and pictures to help you. **Summarize** by telling the important ideas in your own words.

Build Background: Recycle to Make Art

HANDMADE

by Guadalupe Rodríguez

LANDSCAPE
WITH AN ANIMAL

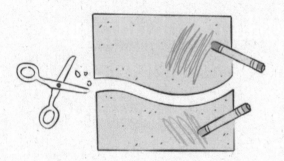

1 On thick paper, draw a curved line. Cut. Color one part the color of the sky. Color the other one like grass or the ocean.

2 Put together the two parts by gluing only the ends. The center part stays open.

3 Get another piece of thick paper. Draw and color an animal. Then cut it out. Cut a strip of thick paper. Glue the end of the strip to the back of the animal. Let it dry.

4 Then put the strip through the open part of the landscape. Attach it with a paper fastener. Make your animal walk along the landscape by moving the strip back and forth.

FLYING
FISH

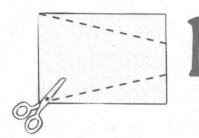 **1** On a large sheet of paper, draw two lines like in the picture. Cut.

 **2** Color the eyes and the body. Glue the edges together.

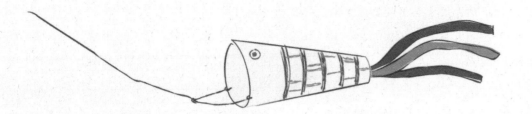

3 Tie a string to both sides of the mouth to make a loop. Tie on a long string to pull. Glue on strips of paper to make the tail.

PAPER
BIRDS

1 Use a plate to `trace` a circle on paper. Cut the circle, and then fold it in half.

2 Draw and cut feathers and a beak out of tissue paper. Glue them on. Then draw an eye on each side of the paper. Get two wooden sticks for the legs. Glue them on.

3 Use thread or yarn to hang up the bird and . . . it'll be ready to fly!

Turn and Talk

Use details from **Handmade** to answer these questions with a partner.

1. Summarize What do you make in each project and how can it be used?

2. Tell the steps for making one of the projects. Use your own words.

Talking Tip

Ask a question if you are not sure about your partner's ideas.

What do you mean by _____?

Write a Letter

PROMPT Pick one of the projects from **Handmade**. Write a letter to tell someone you know how to make it. Use details from **Handmade** to help you explain the steps.

PLAN First, list materials the person will need, like paper. Write about the steps.

First

Next

Last

WRITE Now write a letter to the person. Explain the steps for making the project. Remember to:

- Tell all the materials that are needed.

- Explain the steps in order.

_____

- -

_____

_____

- -

_____

_____

- -

_____

_____

- -

_____

_____

- -

_____

Prepare to Read

GENRE STUDY **Procedural texts** tell how to do or make something.

MAKE A PREDICTION Preview **Be a Bird Helper**. Look at the text features, like the numbers, pictures, and headings, to help you predict. What do you think you will learn?

_____

- -

_____

_____

- -

_____

SET A PURPOSE Read to find out how to help birds and to see if your prediction is right. If not, use the text features to help you make a new prediction as you read.

Be a Bird Helper

READ Why do birds need our help? <u>Underline</u> words that tell.

You Can Help!

Some animals need our help. We can be kind to these animals. Sometimes birds need help in the winter. They cannot find very many things to eat. You can help them get food. Make a bird feeder! ▶

Close Reading Tip

Is your prediction right so far? If not, look at the text features to help you make a new prediction.

CHECK MY UNDERSTANDING

In your own words, what is this part mostly about?

_____

- -

_____

- -

_____

READ <u>Underline</u> words that show the order of the steps. After you read, use your own words to summarize how to make a bird feeder. Tell just the most important ideas.

How to Make a Bird Feeder

💡

Close Reading Tip

Was your prediction about what you would learn correct? What were you right about? What was different?

1 First, ask a grown-up to help you get a pinecone, birdseed, string, stick, and peanut butter or shortening.

2 Next, put shortening or peanut butter on the pinecone. Roll it in the seeds.

3 Then tie string to the pinecone.

4 Last, put the bird feeder in a tree. The birds will thank you by eating the seeds!

CHECK MY UNDERSTANDING

How does the author make the steps easy to understand?

_____

- -

_____

- -

_____

- -

_____

GRAND CANYON

by Sara Gilbert

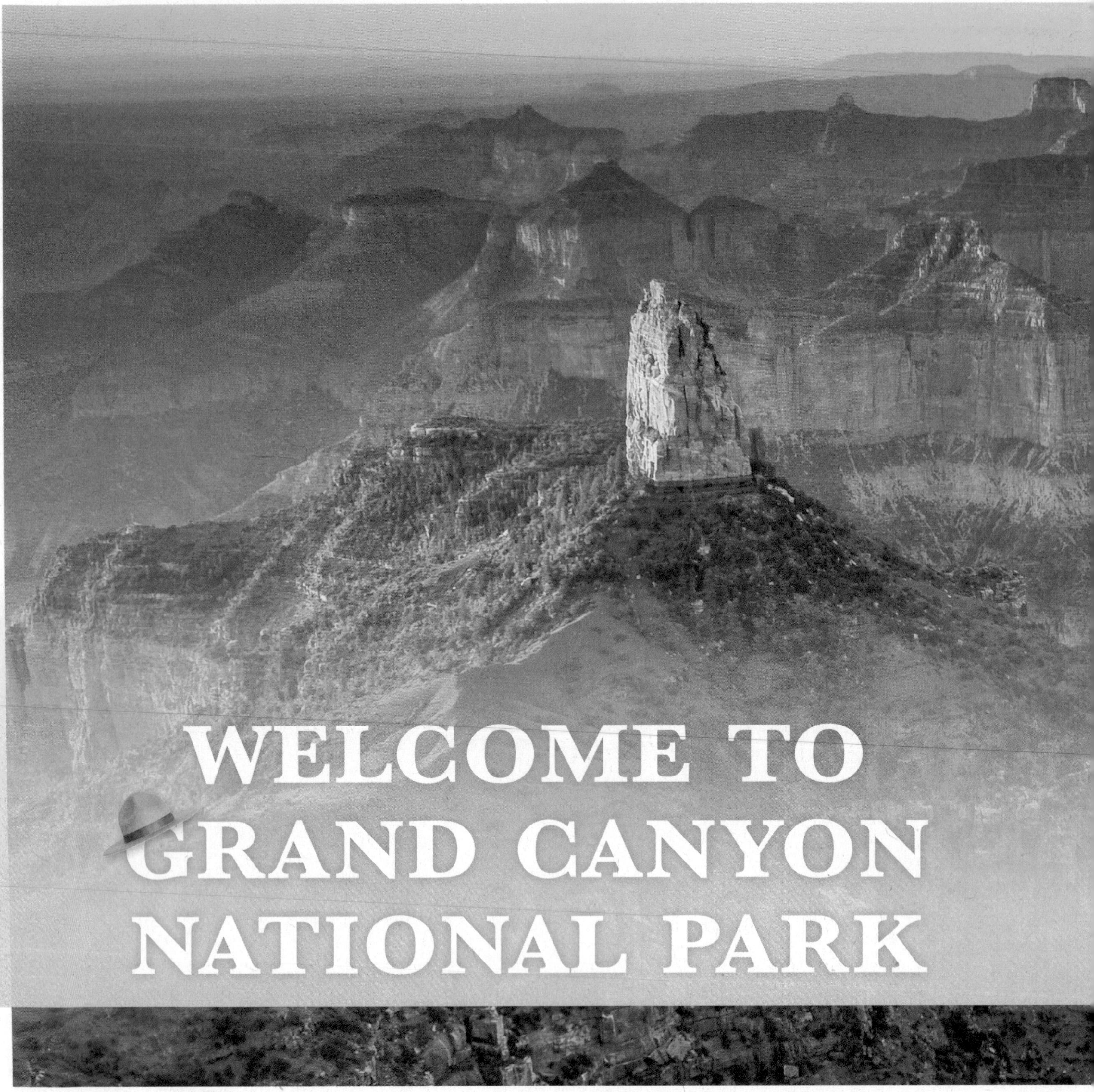

WELCOME TO
GRAND CANYON
NATIONAL PARK

Wow! Look at all that rock! At the Grand
Canyon, you can look deep into the earth.
Some of the rocks are millions of years old.

The Grand Canyon is in Arizona.
It became a national park in 1919.
It is one of the most popular
national parks in the United States.

★ Grand Canyon National Park
■ Arizona

Havasu Creek (below); Pinyon-Juniper Woodlands (next page)

76

ROCKS AND A RIVER

The Grand Canyon covers more than one million acres. Some of it is desert. Other parts have lots of trees. It is cooler in the forests.

The Colorado River runs through the Grand Canyon. It made the canyon walls. The rock layers are different colors. People can find fossils in the rock.

A fern fossil (right); Toroweap Overlook (below)

CANYON CREATURES

More than 500 kinds of animals and birds live here.
The endangered California condor is one of them.
Condors are the biggest birds in North America.

There are about 2,000 kinds of plants in the park. A few are found only in the Grand Canyon. They do not grow anywhere else.

A cactus (right); a white fir tree (below)

BEAUTIFUL VIEWS

Almost 5 million people visit in a year. You can ride a bus around the rim. You can hike down into the canyon. You can even raft on the Colorado River.

It can get very hot in the canyon. Drink lots of water. Look out for wild animals like mountain lions, too. Do not try to feed them!

A mountain lion (below)
Park visitors can see across the canyon for miles. (next page)

Sunset at the Grand Canyon is a special time.
Watch the sun sink below the beautiful rocks!

ACTIVITY

CANYON CREATION

Materials needed:

Sand box or pile of sand

Hose or bucket of water

Step 1: Create a flat, thick area of sand. This will be the earth.

Step 2: Starting at one end of the sand, pour some water on it to make a river. What happens to the sand as the river runs through it?

Step 3: Add more water. Pour some of it quickly and some of it slowly. How does the speed affect what happens to the sand? Does the path of the river change? What happens to the walls around it?

Turn and Talk

GRAND CANYON
by Sara Gilbert

Use details from **Grand Canyon** to answer
these questions with a partner.

1. **Synthesize** What are the most important
   ideas you learned? What makes the
   Grand Canyon seem special to you?

2. Reread the activity on page 84. Describe
   what you think will happen to the sand.

Listening Tip

Listen carefully. Make connections.
How is what your partner says like
other things you know?

Write a Poem

PROMPT   Write a poem about the Grand
Canyon. Use details from **Grand Canyon** to
describe things in an interesting way.

PLAN   Write words that describe the Grand
Canyon or something that lives there. Add
rhyming words and words about the topic.

Describing Words	Rhyming Words	Topic Words
huge	hot – lot – spot	fossils

WRITE Now write a poem to describe the Grand Canyon or something that lives there. Make the poem fun to say and hear! Then recite it for your classmates. You can:

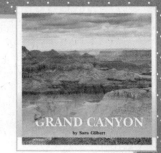

- Use rhyming words and topic words.
- Repeat sounds and words, like **r̲ed r̲ed r̲ocks**.

Prepare to Read

GENRE STUDY **Informational text** is nonfiction.
It gives facts about a topic.

MAKE A PREDICTION Preview **Grand Canyon Fossils**.
Fossils are what is left of living things from
long ago. What do you think you will learn?

_____

_____

_____

_____

SET A PURPOSE Read to find out about fossils in
the Grand Canyon.

Grand Canyon Fossils

READ What is a fossil like? <u>Underline</u> words that tell.

Take a hike in the Grand Canyon and you just may find a fossil! As you walk, look around. You will see all kinds of rocks. Look closer! You see what looks like a shell in the rock. It is very old. You just found a fossil of an animal that lived long ago! ▶

> **Close Reading Tip**
>
> Mark important ideas with *.

CHECK MY UNDERSTANDING

Where can you look for fossils in the Grand Canyon?

_____

_____

_____

_____

READ What kinds of fossils can you find? <u>Underline</u> them. What are the most important ideas you learn about fossils?

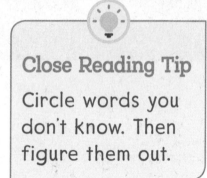

Close Reading Tip

Circle words you don't know. Then figure them out.

Shells are not the only fossils in the Grand Canyon. Long ago, this land was under the water. That's why we can find fossils of sea animals here, like **trilobites**. They look like bugs! You can find fossils of fish, coral, and sea sponges, too.

Plant fossils are also found in the Grand Canyon. Leaves, ferns, and small pine trees all left their prints in the rocks for us to find!

CHECK MY UNDERSTANDING

Use details in the words and photo to describe a **trilobite**.

_____

- -

_____

_____

- -

_____

_____

- -

_____

WRITE ABOUT IT Think about the important ideas from **Grand Canyon Fossils**. What do you think you can learn from looking at fossils? Write sentences to explain your ideas.

Prepare to View

GENRE STUDY **Songs** are words set to music. We can sing them out loud. Listen for:

- what the song is about
- the tune, or how the song sounds
- words or lines that are repeated

SET A PURPOSE Watch the video to find out the main message, or **central idea**, it shares about water. Look and listen for important details that help you understand it.

Build Background: The Water Cycle

WATER CYCLE

by The Bazillions

As You View Listen to the song and look at the pictures. What do you see and hear over and over? Think as you watch. What is the main thing this video is showing you about water? Use details in the words and pictures to figure out this central idea.

Turn and Talk

Use details from **Water Cycle** to answer these questions with a partner.

1. **Central Idea** What is the main thing, or central idea, the video explains about the water cycle?

2. Tell how clouds are an important part of the water cycle.

Talking Tip

Speak loudly enough. Do not speak too fast or too slow.

I think _____ because _____.

Let's Wrap Up!

? Essential Question

How do things in nature change?

Pick one of these activities to show what you have learned about the topic.

1. Recycled Art

Nature changes the Earth and so do people! Make a picture of the Earth using scraps of paper and other things that can be recycled. Write about ways we can take care of our Earth.

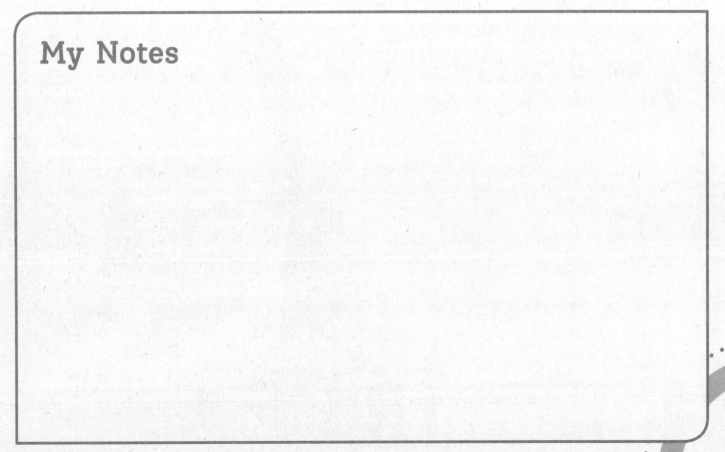

2. Season Expert

Pick a season. Draw
and label a picture of a
place you know in that season.
Tell a partner about the weather
and other changes that happen
in that season.

Word Challenge

Can you use the
word cycle to help
explain what
happens?

My Notes

Tell Me a Story

"Lessons learned when you are young last a lifetime."

—Hispanic Proverb

What lessons can we learn from stories?

Get Curious
Video

Words About What Stories Teach Us

Complete the Vocabulary Network to show what you know about the words.

literature

Meaning: Stories, plays, and poems are all kinds of **literature**.

Synonyms and Antonyms	Drawing

entertain

Meaning: When you want to **entertain** people, you could act, sing, or dance.

Synonyms and Antonyms	Drawing

amuse

Meaning: If you **amuse** people, you make them smile or laugh.

Synonyms and Antonyms	Drawing

Short Read

READ Together

Follow the Story Path

What are the parts of a story? Follow the path to find out.

CHARACTERS

Characters are the people or animals in a story.

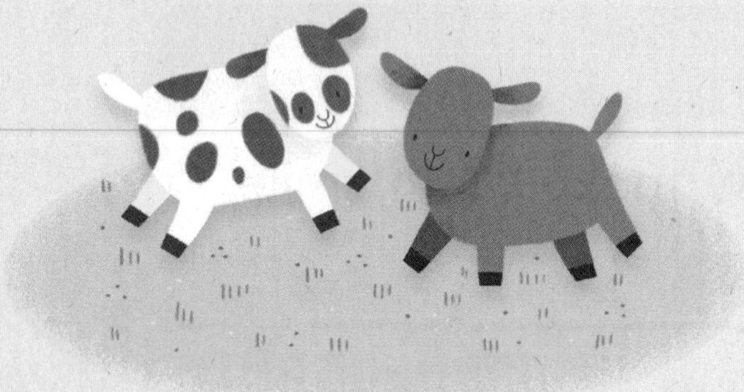

SETTING

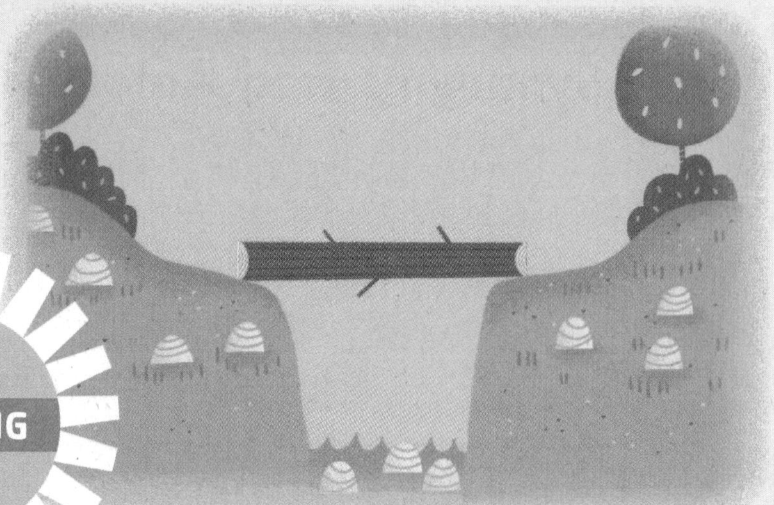

The **setting** is where and when the story happens.

BEGINNING

The events in the **beginning** tell what the **problem** is. The problem is what goes wrong.

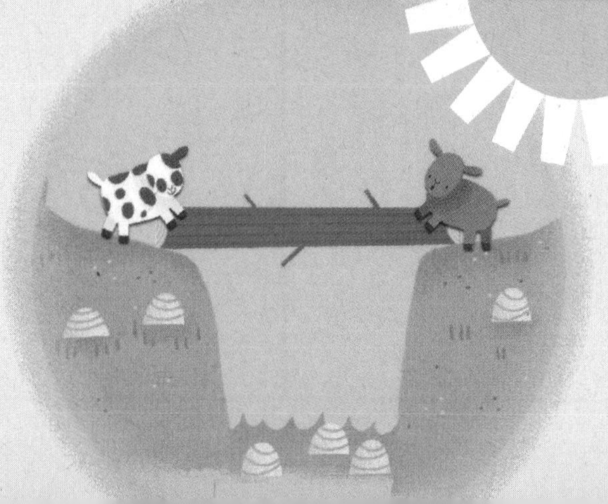

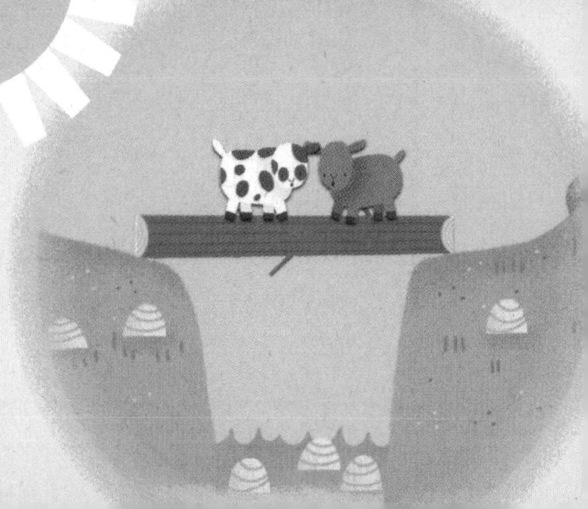

MIDDLE

The events in the middle tell how the characters try to solve the problem.

END

The events at the end tell the **resolution**, or how the problem is solved.

Now follow the path again. Tell your own version of the story of the two goats! Use the pictures for help.

Prepare to Read

GENRE STUDY **Fantasy** stories have made-up events that could not really happen. Look for:

- animal characters that act like people
- short tales within this story
- a problem and a resolution

SET A PURPOSE Make pictures in your mind as you read. Words that tell how things look, sound, feel, taste, or smell and words about feelings help you **create mental images**.

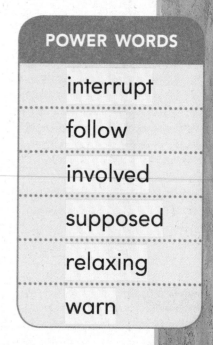

POWER WORDS

interrupt

follow

involved

supposed

relaxing

warn

Meet David Ezra Stein.

INTERRUPTING CHICKEN

by David Ezra Stein

It was bedtime for the little red chicken.

"Okay, my little chicken," said Papa.
"Are you all ready to go to sleep?"

"Yes, Papa! But you forgot something."

"What's that?" asked Papa.

"A bedtime story!"

"All right," said Papa. "I'll read one of your favorites. And of course you are not going to *interrupt* the story tonight, are you?"

"Oh no, Papa, I'll be good."

Hansel and Gretel were very hungry. Deep in the woods they found a house made of candy. Nibble, nibble, nibble; they began to eat the house, until the old woman who lived there came out and said, "What lovely children! Why don't you come inside?" They were just about to follow her when—

Out jumped a little red chicken, and she said,
"DON'T GO IN! SHE'S A WITCH!"
KID
SOUP

So Hansel and Gretel didn't.
THE END!

"Chicken."

"Yes, Papa?"

"You interrupted the story. Try not to get so involved."

"I'm sorry, Papa. But she really was a witch."

"Well, you're supposed to be relaxing so you can fall asleep."

"Let's try another story. I'll be good!"

"Take this basket of goodies to Grandma," said Little Red Riding Hood's mother. "But don't stray from the path. The woods are full of danger." Red Riding Hood skipped along through the deep woods. By and by she met a wolf who wished her "Good morning." She was about to answer him when—

Out jumped a little red chicken, and she said,
"DON'T TALK TO STRANGERS!"

So Little Red Riding Hood didn't.
THE END!

"Chicken."

"Yes, Papa?"

"You did it again. You interrupted two stories, and you're not even sleepy!"

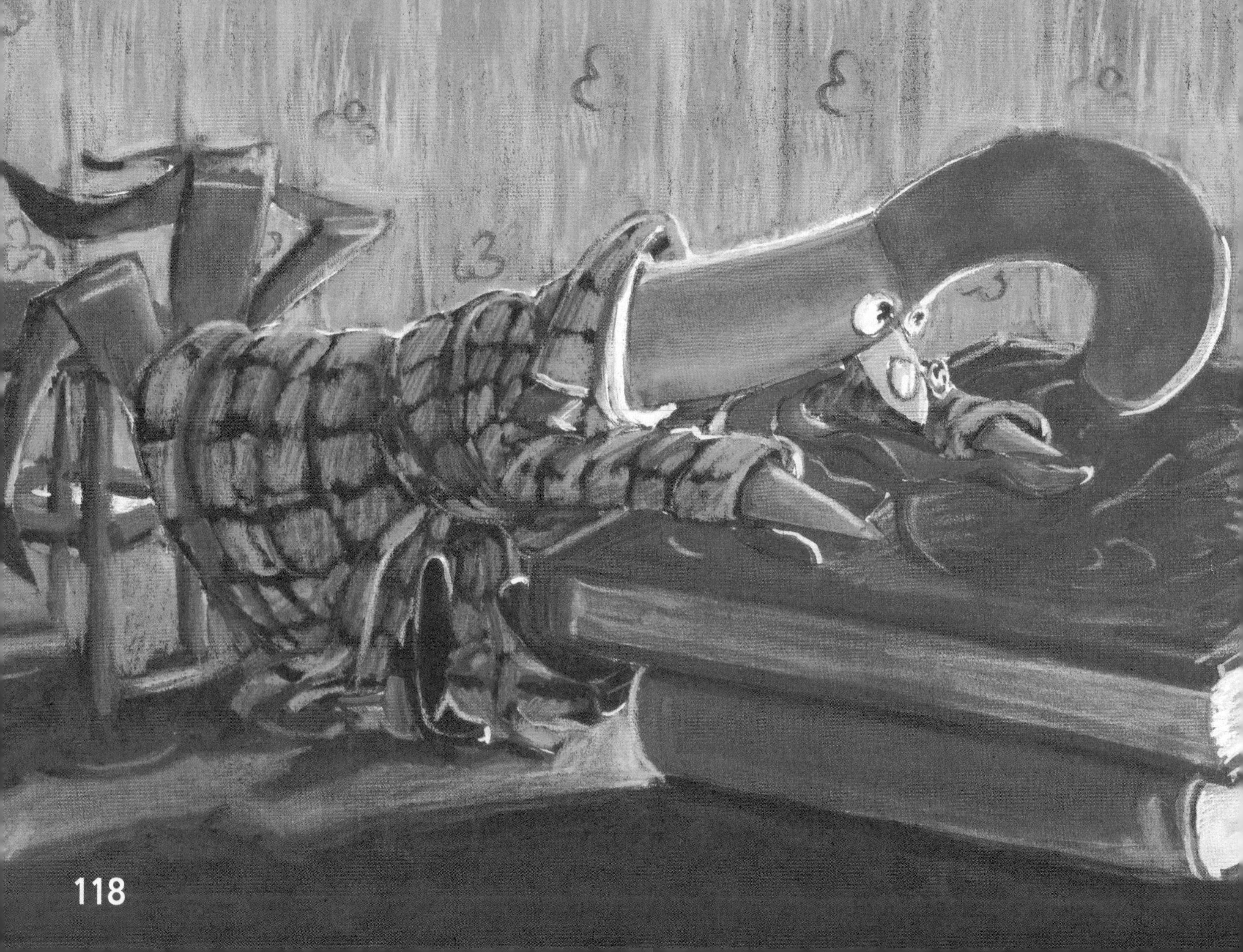

"I know, Papa! I'm sorry. But he was a *mean* old wolf."

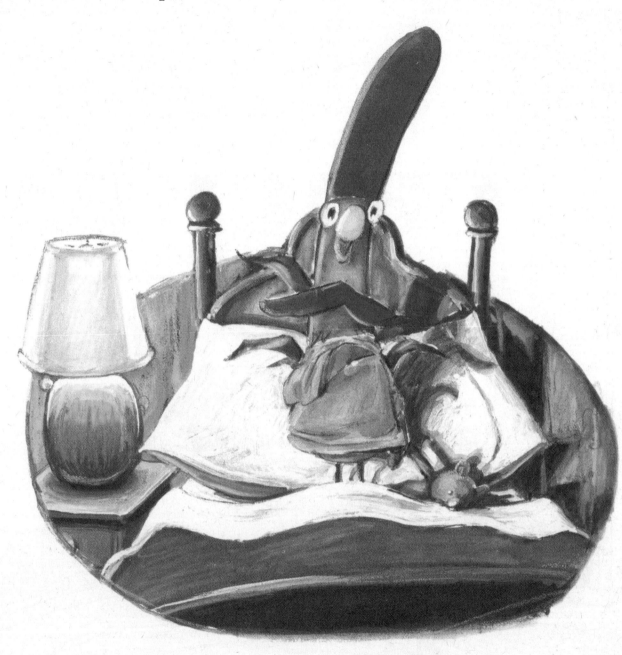

"Yes. Now get back into bed."

"Okay, Papa. Let's try one more *little* story, and I'll be good!"

120

Chicken Little was hit on the head by an acorn. *The sky is falling!* she thought. She was about to run off and warn Goosey Loosey, Ducky Lucky, Henny Penny, and everyone on the farm the sky was falling when—

Out jumped a little red chicken, and she said,
"DON'T PANIC! IT WAS JUST AN ACORN."

123

"Chicken."

"Yes, Papa?"

"You did it AGAIN."

"Oh, Papa. I couldn't let that little chicken get all upset over an acorn! Please read *one more* story, and I promise I'll fall asleep."

124

"But Chicken," said Papa, "we are out of stories."

"Oh no, Papa. I can't go to sleep without a story!"

"Then," said Papa, yawning, "why don't you tell *me* a story?"

"*Me* tell a story?" said the little red chicken. "Okay, Papa! Here we go! Um . . ."

Once there was a little red chicken who put her Papa to bed. She read him a hundred stories. She even gave him warm milk, but nothing worked: he stayed wide awake all—

"Papa?"

"Good night, Papa."

THE END

Turn and Talk

Use details from **Interrupting Chicken** to answer these questions with a partner.

1. **Create Mental Images** What pictures did you create in your mind when Chicken interrupted each story? Which words helped you create those pictures?

2. Tell why the ending of the story is funny.

Talking Tip

Wait for your turn to speak. Explain your ideas and feelings clearly.

I think _____ because _____.

Write a Story

PROMPT   Look back at the bedtime story
about Chicken Little in **Interrupting Chicken**.
Tell that story in your own way.

PLAN First, write your ideas for the
beginning, middle, and end of the story.

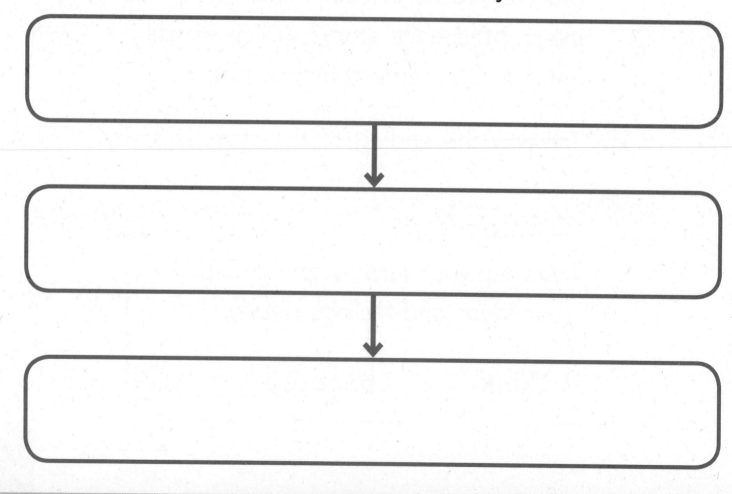

WRITE Now write your story about Chicken Little. Use your own words. Remember to:

- Tell the beginning, middle, and end.

- Use words like **first**, **next**, and **last** to show the order of the events that happen.

Prepare to Read

GENRE STUDY **Fantasy** stories have made-up events that could not really happen.

MAKE A PREDICTION Preview **Hansel and Gretel Two**. Think about how a fantasy has make-believe events. What do you think will happen?

_____

_____

_____

_____

_____

_____

SET A PURPOSE Read to find out what Hansel and Gretel do and to see if your prediction is right. If not, make a new prediction.

Hansel and Gretel Two

READ Describe what Hansel and Gretel are doing. Tell why.

One day, we were hiking in the forest.

"Hansel, look! That little house over there has shiny red and yellow candy all over it," said Gretel. "Yum! I'm hungry."

"I'm hungry, too! Let's take a nibble," I said. Just then, out jumped a little chicken! ▶

Close Reading Tip

Is your prediction right so far? If not, think about the genre and make a new prediction.

CHECK MY UNDERSTANDING

Which words help you picture what the house is like?

_____

- - - - - - - - - - - - - - - - - - - -

_____

- - - - - - - - - - - - - - - - - - - -

_____

135

READ Why do the children invite the chicken to their house? <u>Underline</u> words that tell.

Close Reading Tip

Write **C** when you make a connection.

"DON'T EAT THAT! IT'S NOT GOOD FOR YOUR TEETH!" the little chicken yelled.

We decided that this funny chicken was just trying to help us and so must be nice.

"Do you want to come to our house to play?" I asked the little chicken.

"Is it made of candy?" she asked with a grin. And we all hiked off together!

CHECK MY UNDERSTANDING

Describe what Hansel and Gretel are like. How do you know?

_____

_____

_____

_____

_____

_____

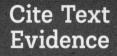

WRITE ABOUT IT How are the things that Hansel and Gretel do in this new story different from what they did in **Interrupting Chicken**? Write to explain.

Guided
Practice

READ
Together

Prepare to Read

GENRE STUDY **Dramas** are stories that are read and acted out. Look for:

- a setting where the story takes place
- dialogue, or what the characters say
- a narrator called the Storyteller

SET A PURPOSE As you read, **make connections** by finding ways that this text is like things in your life and other texts you have read. This will help you understand and remember the text.

POWER WORDS
storyteller
sly
boldly

Meet Lisa Campbell Ernst.

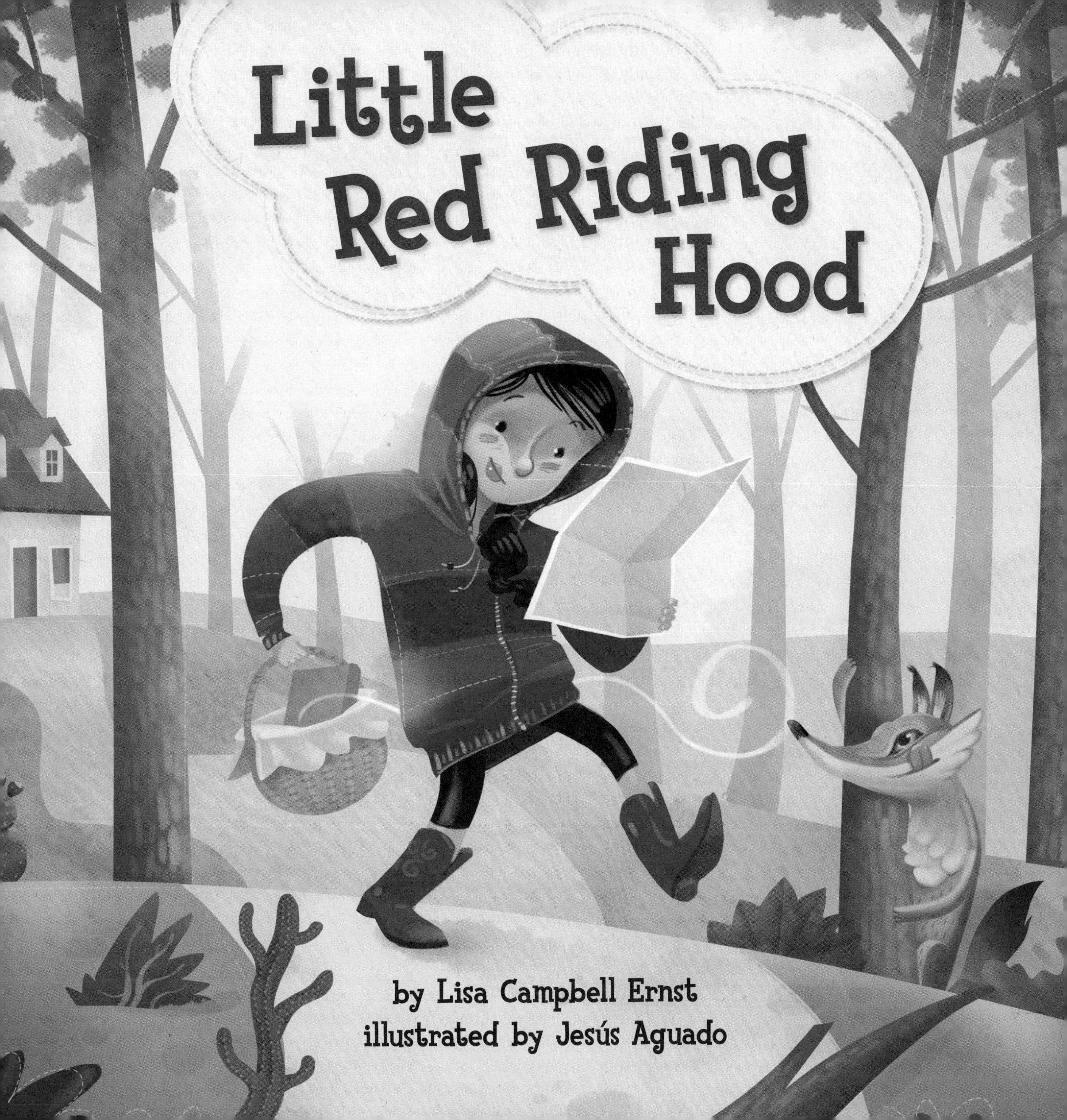

Little Red Riding Hood

by Lisa Campbell Ernst

illustrated by Jesús Aguado

Cast:

Storyteller

Little Red Riding Hood

Mamá

Coyote

Abuela

Storyteller: Once upon a time, there was a girl named Little Red Riding Hood. She lived with her family in a cozy house near the deep, dark woods.

Mamá: Little Red Riding Hood, your grandmother is sick. I'm making fresh, tasty tortillas. Will you please take them to Abuela?

Little Red Riding Hood: Yahoo! Abuela loves tortillas! I'll bring a book to read to her, too. I'll leave right now.

Mamá: Slow down, dear! Here's a map that shows the path to Abuela's house. Stay on the path, and please be careful.

Little Red Riding Hood: This map shows that it's close by. I'll stay on the path. I'll be fine.

Map to Abuela's House

Storyteller: So Little Red Riding Hood headed off to Abuela's house. The tortillas were still nice and warm. Hungry Coyote was close by in the woods.

Coyote: Oooh la la! What is that I smell? My nose tells me it's oh so good!

Storyteller: Coyote sniffed and sniffed. The smell led him to Little Red Riding Hood.

Coyote: Well, hi there! Who are you, and where are you going on this fine day?

Little Red Riding Hood: I'm Little Red Riding Hood. I'm taking tortillas to my sick grandmother. This is my map. It shows me the way.

Storyteller: Hungry Coyote looked at the map and got a mean idea. He had a sly smile on his face.

Coyote: Look at these nice flowers! Flowers might help your grandmother feel better. Why don't you pick some?

Little Red Riding Hood: Thanks for the idea! I'll pick some bright flowers for Abuela.

Storyteller: While Little Red Riding Hood picked a bunch of the best flowers, Coyote ran off. He ran along the path, right to Abuela's house.

Coyote: Hee hee hee! I'm so sly! I'll steal all the tortillas!

Storyteller: Coyote knocked on the door. He spoke in a high voice.

Coyote: Hi, Abuela! It's me, Little Red Riding Hood!

Abuela: Please come in, my dear.

Storyteller: Coyote leaped in. He boldly locked Abuela in a closet. Then he put on a dress and hat to look like her. Soon, Little Red Riding Hood was outside. She knocked.

Little Red Riding Hood: Hi, Abuela, it's me! I have tortillas, flowers, and a book to help you feel better!

Storyteller: Coyote tried to speak in a voice like Abuela's.

Coyote: Come in, sweet Little Red Riding Hood.

Storyteller: Little Red Riding Hood stepped inside. Abuela did not seem like herself.

Little Red Riding Hood: My, Abuela, your eyes are so big!

Coyote: So I can see you, my dear.

Little Red Riding Hood: My, Abuela, your ears are so big!

Coyote: So I can hear you read to me, my dear.

Little Red Riding Hood: My, Abuela, your teeth are so big!

Coyote: So I can eat ALL of your tortillas!

Storyteller: Coyote jumped up! He got stuck once or twice but got the dress and hat off at last.

Storyteller: Just then, Little Red Riding Hood got a text message.

Little Red Riding Hood: Wait just a minute…

Storyteller: She read the message out loud.

Little Red Riding Hood: *I'm in the closet. Please let me out! Love, Abuela.*

Storyteller: Brave Little Red Riding Hood dashed to the closet and unlocked it. In a flash, Abuela jumped out.

Abuela: What's going on in here?

Little Red Riding Hood: This mean Coyote wants to steal the tortillas!

Coyote: I'm not mean! I'm just so hungry! Please FEED me. PLEASE!

Abuela: Come with us, Coyote.

Storyteller: They led Coyote to the kitchen. He sat down with a big sigh.

Little Red Riding Hood: All you had to do was ask, Coyote. We like to share our tortillas!

Storyteller: They all ate the tasty tortillas together. Little Red Riding Hood read to Abuela. She felt better, and so did Coyote. Now we come to the end of our tale of a brave girl, her Abuela, and one very hungry Coyote!

Use details from **Little Red Riding Hood** to answer these questions with a partner.

1. **Make Connections** How is this story of Little Red Riding Hood like the one in **Interrupting Chicken**? How is it different?

2. Why does Little Red Riding Hood change the way she feels about Coyote during the story?

Listening Tip

Look at your partner. Listen politely and think about what your partner is saying.

Write a Drama

PROMPT Where will the characters from **Little Red Riding Hood** go next? Write a short drama to add on to the story.

PLAN First, draw a picture of what is happening in your new scene.

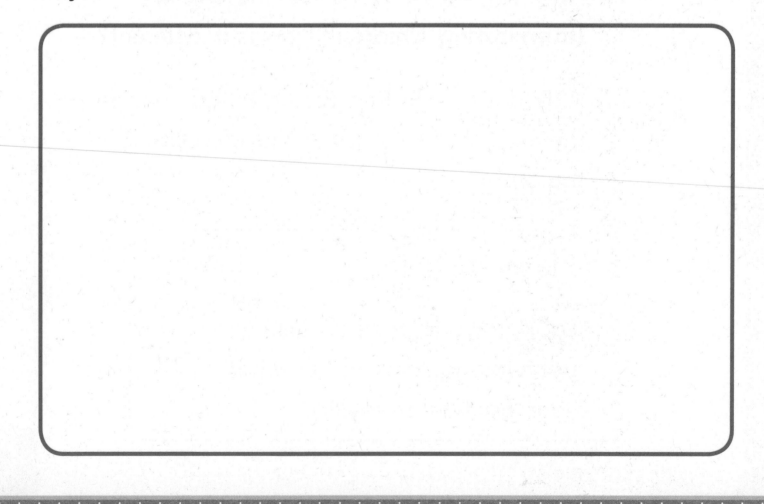

WRITE Now write your short drama. Tell what everyone says and does. Use another sheet of paper if you need to. Then share it with classmates. Tell them what things about your writing make it a drama. Remember to:

- Begin with a list of the **characters**.

- Name the place and describe this **setting**.

- Make the **dialogue** sound like real talking.

Prepare to Read

GENRE STUDY **Dramas** are stories that are read and acted out.

MAKE A PREDICTION Preview **Keep Trying**. A girl is trying to learn how to ride a bike. What do you think will happen?

_____

- -

_____

- -

_____

- -

_____

SET A PURPOSE Read to find out if the girl learns to ride her bike.

Keep Trying

READ **READ** Who is in this drama? <u>Underline</u> the characters' names.

Cast: **Narrator** **June** **Max**

Narrator: June is learning to ride a bike in the park. Her big brother is helping her.

June: I'll never learn how to ride this bike. I think I'm going to fall!

Max: Just keep trying, June! ▶

Close Reading Tip
Write **C** when you make a connection.

CHECK MY UNDERSTANDING

Describe the setting where the drama takes place.

_____

_____

_____

READ What does the dialogue tell you about June?

Close Reading Tip

Put a ! by a surprising part.

Narrator: June didn't learn at first, but she didn't give up.

Max: You're getting better. You're almost ready to take off by yourself, June.

June: OK, Max, I'm ready. Let go!

Narrator: June started to fall! But she didn't. She learned an important lesson. If you can't do something at first, keep trying!

CHECK MY UNDERSTANDING

How are **Keep Trying** and **Little Red Riding Hood** alike?

_____

- -

_____

_____

- -

_____

_____

- -

_____

160

WRITE ABOUT IT How does June learn a lesson in **Keep Trying**? Use examples from the drama to explain your answer.

_____

- -

_____

- -

_____

- -

_____

- -

_____

- -

_____

- -

_____

- -

_____

- -

_____

- -

_____

- -

Prepare to Read

GENRE STUDY ▶ **Fables** have been told for many years and teach a lesson. Look for:

- animals that are characters
- how the pictures and words help you understand what happens

SET A PURPOSE ▶ Read to make smart guesses, or **inferences**, about things the author does not say. Use what you already know and clues in the text and pictures to help you.

POWER WORDS

labor

chirped

autumn

Meet Jerry Pinkney.

162

THE GRASSHOPPER & THE ANTS

by Jerry Pinkney

"Why work so hard?"
sang Grasshopper.
"It's spring and time to go fishing."

"No time to relax,"
said the Ants.

"Why labor so long?"
Grasshopper chirped. "It's summertime.
Let's have a picnic of fresh, yummy leaves.
Come join me in making music!"

"No summer light to waste," replied the Ants. "Autumn will be here soon."

"Why toil so steady?" asked Grasshopper.
"It's fall and the world is a playground of leaves.
Oh, how their colors twirl and glide!
Come dance and sing!"

"Look at this wonderful mountain of leaves. Come play!"

"And oh, how I love the sparkle
of first snow. Come see!"

"Working can wait,"
Grasshopper said.

"Wintertime is for making snow angels
and snow-hoppers."

171

"If only someone would join me!"
Grasshopper shivered.

178

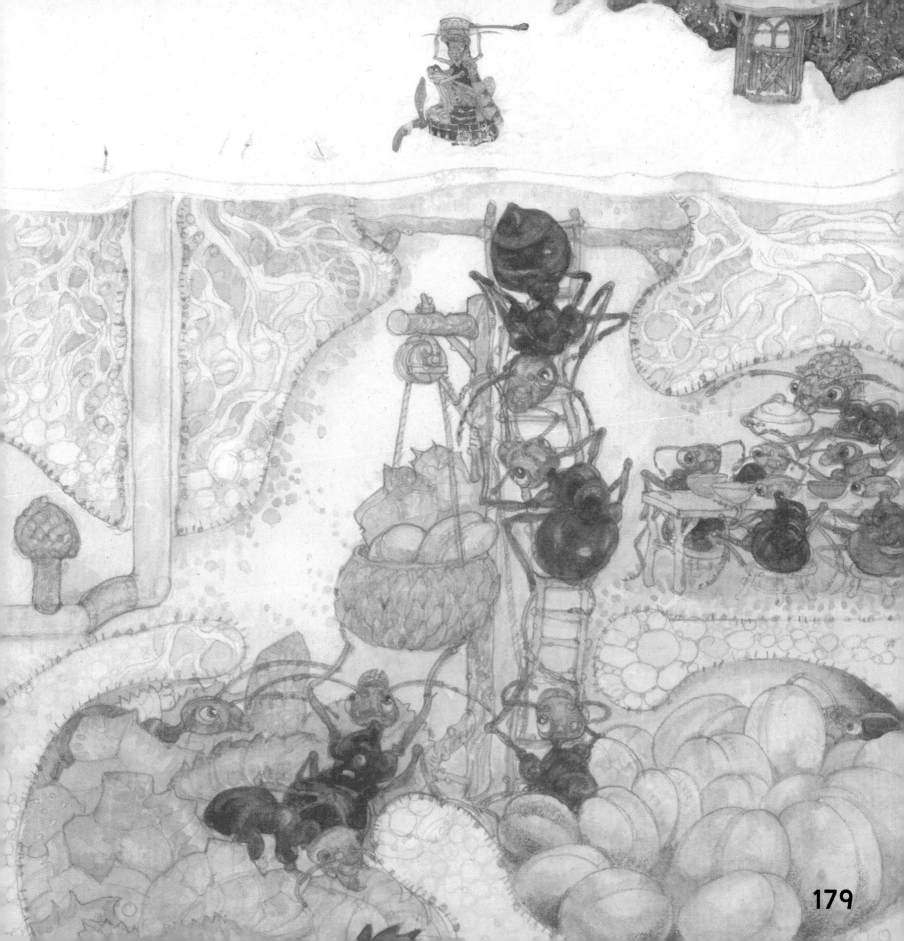

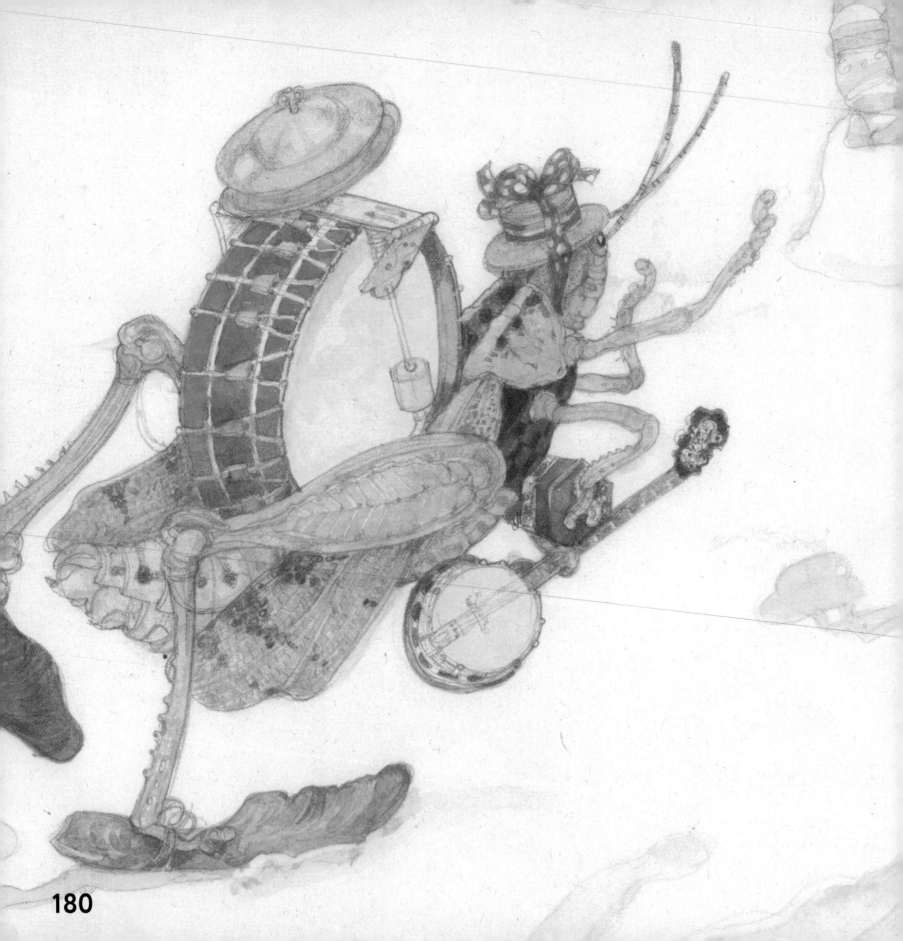

"A cup of tea?" asked Queen Ant.
"How kind of you," said Grasshopper.

183

Turn and Talk

Use details from **The Grasshopper & the Ants**
to answer these questions with a partner.

1. **Make Inferences** What do Grasshopper
and the Ants learn from each other?

2. Do you think the Ants should share with
Grasshopper? Why or why not?

Talking Tip

Complete the sentence to add to
what your partner says.

My idea is _____.

Write a Description

PROMPT How does Grasshopper change during the story? Use details from the words and pictures to explain your ideas.

PLAN Describe what Grasshopper is like at the beginning, middle, and end of the story.

Beginning	Middle	End

WRITE Now write sentences to describe how Grasshopper changes. Remember to:

- Tell about Grasshopper's actions and feelings at the beginning, middle, and end of the story.

- Use describing words.

Prepare to Read

GENRE STUDY **Fables** have been told for many years and teach a lesson.

MAKE A PREDICTION Preview **A Tale of Two Mice**. You know fables teach a lesson. What lesson do you think the mice will learn in this fable?

_____

- - - - - - - - - - - - - - - - - -

_____

_____

- - - - - - - - - - - - - - - - - -

_____

_____

- - - - - - - - - - - - - - - - - -

SET A PURPOSE Read to find out what happens when the mice visit each other and to see if your prediction is right.

ZOOM

beep!
beep!

A Tale of Two Mice

READ What is the city like? <u>Underline</u> words that describe it.

Country Mouse got an e-mail from his friend. "Come visit me in the city!" it said.

So Country Mouse took a bike, a bus, and a train. At last, he got to the big city. It was so busy! People rushed past. Loud horns honked. Country Mouse was scared! ▶

Close Reading Tip

Is your prediction right so far? If not, think about what fables are like and make a new prediction.

CHECK MY UNDERSTANDING

Describe the city and how Country Mouse feels about it.

_____

- -

_____

- -

_____

189

Close Reading Tip

Put a ! by a surprising part.

Country Mouse texted City Mouse. "I'm going home! Please come visit *me!*"

So City Mouse took a train, a bus, and a bike. When he got to the country, he saw no one. It was silent. He felt nervous.

City Mouse texted his friend. "This place is too quiet for me! Why don't we meet someplace in the middle?"

CHECK MY UNDERSTANDING

Why does City Mouse want to meet Country Mouse someplace in the middle?

_____

_____

_____

_____

_____

_____

WRITE ABOUT IT What lesson do you think the
mice learn? Write sentences to tell about it.

_____

- -

_____

_____

- -

_____

_____

- -

_____

_____

- -

_____

_____

- -

_____

_____

- -

_____

191

Prepare to Read

GENRE STUDY **Informational text** is nonfiction. It gives facts about a topic. Look for:

- facts about people
- photographs of real people

SET A PURPOSE Read to find out the most important ideas in each part. Then **synthesize**, or put the ideas together in your mind, to find out new things about the text and what it really means to you.

Meet Helen Lester.

Thank You, Mr. Aesop

by Helen Lester

illustrated by
Roberto Weigand

Aesop lived a long, long time ago. It was SO LONG AGO that we are not even sure he was real! Some people think Aesop was a storyteller from Greece who told stories about animals that acted like people. Some animals were full of nonsense. Others were wise.

These stories are called *fables*. Each one teaches a lesson.

People liked Aesop's fables. One person told the story to another . . . who told another . . . who told another. . . . You get the idea!

Long after Aesop's time, people were still telling the fables. They were printed in books. Each author changed the story to make it a little different.

Today, people still like Aesop's fables! Many authors retell these stories. The author Jerry Pinkney wrote his own versions of Aesop's fables. His art helps to tell each tale.

Ed Emberley and his daughter Rebecca also retell Aesop's fables. They change the stories to make them their own. In their book The Ant and the Grasshopper, the weather is hot, not cold like in other versions. Also, the grasshopper is not alone. He plays music with a bug band!

Think of it! Many fables we know were first told long, LONG ago. These stories hold lessons for us all.

So, will YOU be the next storyteller? I hope your reply is "Yes!" You could retell an old fable or make up a new one. What lesson will it teach?

Turn and Talk

Thank You, Mr. Aesop

Use details from **Thank You, Mr. Aesop** to answer these questions with a partner.

1. **Synthesize** Why do you think Aesop's fables have been told over and over for so long?

2. How are Jerry Pinkney's stories different from Aesop's?

Talking Tip

Ask a question if you are not sure about your partner's ideas.

Why did you say _____?

Write Facts

PROMPT What are the most interesting facts you learned from **Thank You, Mr. Aesop**? Look back at the sentences and pictures for ideas.

PLAN First, write notes about the facts, or true information, you learned about Aesop, fables, and authors.

WRITE Now write three of the most interesting facts you learned from **Thank You, Mr. Aesop**. Remember to:

- Tell true information.

- Make sure each sentence tells a complete idea and ends with an end mark.

Prepare to Read

Informational text is nonfiction. It gives facts about a topic.

Preview **Make Stories Come Alive**. You know that an informational text has facts. What do you think you will learn?

_____

_____

_____

_____

_____

Read to find out how to tell a story for others to enjoy.

Make Stories Come Alive

READ What do storytellers do? <u>Underline</u> the words that tell.

Do you know a good storyteller? Good storytellers make you want to listen. They can make you laugh. They tell stories that make you feel excited, sad, or scared.

Telling a story isn't hard! You can do it, too. It just takes time and some practice. ▶

Close Reading Tip

Mark important ideas with *.

CHECK MY UNDERSTANDING

What is the most important thing you learn on this page?

_____

_____

_____

_____

203

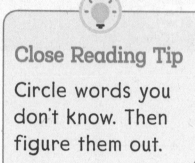

Close Reading Tip

Circle words you don't know. Then figure them out.

READ Which details tell how to be a good storyteller? <u>Underline</u> them.

Here are some storytelling tips. First, pick a story you like. Then tell it out loud. Speak clearly. Use different voices for the characters. You can also use your body to act out the story. Practice telling it a few times.

Then share your story. You could tell it to a group or make a video for people to watch. Make it funny or exciting! Remember to have fun. Make your story come alive!

CHECK MY UNDERSTANDING

What is the main idea, or central idea, of the whole text?

_____

- -

_____

_____

- -

_____

_____

- -

_____

WRITE ABOUT IT Write the title of a story you
would like to tell. Then write things you learned that
you will do to make your story lively and exciting
when you tell it.

_____

- -

_____

- -

_____

- -

_____

- -

_____

- -

_____

- -

_____

- -

_____

- -

_____

Prepare to View

GENRE STUDY **Videos** are short movies. Some videos give information. Others are for you to watch for enjoyment. Watch and listen for:

- the lesson the video teaches
- how the pictures, words, and sounds work together to tell a story

SET A PURPOSE Watch to find out who the **characters** are and what they look like. Find out what the characters do, say, and feel to help you understand why they act as they do.

Build Background: Tortoises and Hares

The Tortoise and the Hare

START

from Speakaboos, adapted by Amy Kraft

As You View Use the pictures and words to find out what the tortoise and hare are like. What do they do? Look for details to help you understand why the characters act the way they do. What lessons do they learn?

A whistle blew, and they were off. The hare sprinted down the road while the tortoise crawled away from the starting line.

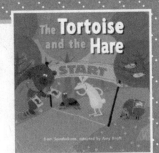

Turn and Talk

Use details from **The Tortoise and the Hare** to answer these questions with a partner.

1. Characters Describe the hare. Why does the hare stop to rest during the race?

2. What lesson does the hare learn after the race?

Talking Tip

Speak loudly enough so that your partner can hear you. Do not speak too fast or too slow.

I think that _____.

READ
Together

Let's Wrap Up!

(?) **Essential Question**

What lessons can we learn from stories?

....

Pick one of these activities to show what
you have learned about the topic.

1. Make a Badge

Make a badge. Draw a picture
on it that shows a lesson you
learned from the stories.
Write a sentence to tell
how to earn the badge.

2. Guessing Game

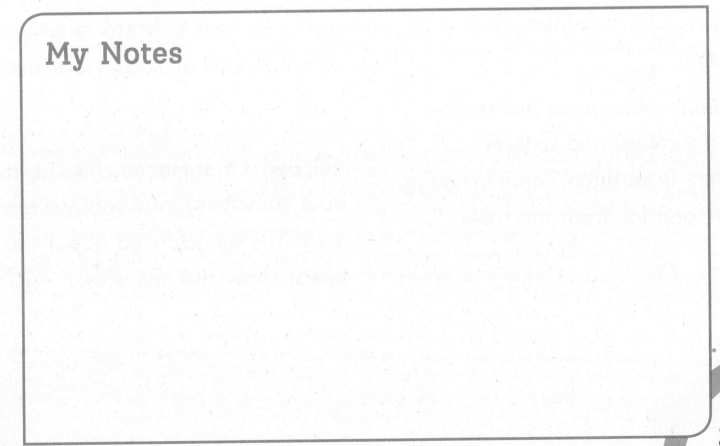

Choose a character from the stories. Think about the lesson the character learned. Act out something the character would do. Have a partner guess the character.

Word Challenge

Can you use the word amuse to tell about the character?

My Notes

Glossary

A

affect If things affect something else, they change it in some way. How does the hot sun **affect** how you feel?

amuse If you amuse people, you make them smile or laugh. We did a funny play to **amuse** our parents.

autumn Autumn is the season after summer and before winter. In **autumn**, leaves change color and fall from the trees.

B

boldly If you do something boldly, you do it in a way that is confident or not polite. She **boldly** took the toy when it was not her turn to use it.

break A break is a short rest. We took a **break** after working hard at soccer practice.

C

chirped If someone chirped, they said something in a happy, lively way. The girl **chirped** about the great show she just saw.

cycle A cycle is a group of events that repeat in the same order. The seasons come one after another in a **cycle**.

D

direction A direction is the certain way or path that someone goes along. When we went hiking, we walked in the **direction** of the lake.

dunes Dunes are hills of sand in a desert or by the ocean. We walked up and down the sand **dunes** at the beach.

E

edges The edges of something are the places where it ends. The two teams stood along the **edges** of the field.

entertain When you want to entertain people, you could act, sing, or dance. The children **entertain** us by dancing in the parade.

evaporation Evaporation is when a liquid turns into a gas. After the storm, **evaporation** made the water puddles go away.

F

follow   When you follow someone, you walk behind that person to go to the same place. Baby ducks **follow** their mother to the pond.

fossils   Fossils are what is left of plants and animals from long ago and can be found in rocks. Some **fossils** are dinosaur bones or look like shells or leaves.

H

hike   When you hike, you go on a long walk. It takes a long time to **hike** to the lake.

I

interrupt   When you interrupt someone, you stop that person from talking. If you **interrupt** me, I won't be able to tell you the rest of the story.

involved   If you are involved in something, you join in and feel strongly about it. He got **involved** in telling a story to us and made it exciting.

L

labor   When you labor, you work When we **labor** in the garden, we pull weeds and water the plants.

landed If something landed, it came down to the ground. The jet **landed** at the airport.

lesson A lesson is something important you learn. We learned a **lesson** about why it is good to share.

liquid A liquid is something that you can pour, like water or milk. I pour the **liquid** to fill up each part.

literature Stories, plays, and poems are all kinds of literature. My teacher gives us good **literature** to read.

M

mission A mission is an important job you do. Our **mission** is to paint the fence.

N

nonsense If something is nonsense, it is silly or not true. The silly fox in the story was full of **nonsense**.

P

popular If something is popular, many people know about it and like it. All of us want to play the **popular** game.

problem   A problem is something that is hard to figure out. The dog's **problem** is that it cannot reach the ball.

R

relaxing   When you are relaxing, you are resting. After work, he is **relaxing** at his house.

reply   A reply is an answer to a question. My **reply** to your question is "Yes!"

rest   When you rest, you are quiet, don't do anything, and might sleep. We **rest** after playing all day.

rim   A rim is the place where something ends, or the edge of it. We walk along the **rim** and see a river down below.

S

shrubs   Shrubs are bushes, which are woody plants with lots of stems and are smaller than trees. We planted small **shrubs** by our house.

sly   A person who is sly is smart and might have a secret. In the story, the tricky fox had a **sly** look on its face.

spectacular   If something is spectacular, it is very big and exciting to look at. That **spectacular** waterfall is so big!

spines If something has spines, it has thin, pointed parts that are sharp. Don't touch the sharp **spines** on the cactus plant!

storyteller A storyteller is a person who writes or tells a story. The **storyteller** told a funny story to our class.

supposed If you are supposed to do something, you should do it. We are **supposed** to do our homework.

T

tale A tale is a story. We read a **tale** about a little red hen.

trace To trace something, you draw a line around the outside of it. **Trace** around your hand to make a picture of your hand.

W

warn When you warn people, you let them know about danger. The police officer will **warn** drivers if the roads get icy.

wise If you are wise, you use what you know to make good decisions. The **wise** leader helped us pick the best place to camp.

Index of Titles and Authors

Acknowledgments

Cover illustration from *The Ant and the Grasshopper* by Rebecca Emberley and Ed Emberley. Copyright © 2012 by Rebecca Emberley Inc. Reprinted by permission of Macmillan Publishing Company.

Cover illustration from *The Crocodile and the Scorpion* by Rebecca Emberley and Ed Emberley. Copyright © 2013 by Rebecca Emberley and Ed Emberley. Reprinted by permission of Roaring Brook Press, a division of Holtzbrinck Publishing Holdings Limited Partnership.

Cover illustration from *The Lion & the Mouse* by Jerry Pinkney. Copyright © 2009 by Jerry Pinkney. Reprinted by permission of Little, Brown Books for Young Readers, a division of Hachette Book Group, Inc.

Cover illustration from *The Tortoise & the Hare* by Jerry Pinkney. Copyright © 2013 by Jerry Pinkney. Reprinted by permission of Little, Brown Books for Young Readers, a division of Hachette Book Group, Inc.

Deserts by Quinn M. Arnold. Text copyright © 2017 by Creative Education and Creative Paperbacks. Creative Education and Creative Paperbacks are imprints of The Creative Company, Mankato, MN 56001 USA. Reprinted by permission of The Creative Company.

Grand Canyon by Sara Gilbert. Text copyright © 2017 by Sara Gilbert. Reprinted by permission of Creative Education, an imprint of The Creative Company, Mankato, MN 56001 USA.

The Grasshopper and the Ants by Jerry Pinkney. Copyright © 2015 by Jerry Pinkney. Published by Little, Brown Books for Young Readers. Reprinted by permission of Little, Brown and Company and Sheldon Fogelman Agency, Inc.

"Landscape with an Animal" (retitled from "Paisaje con animal"), "Flying Fish" (retitled from "Pez volador"), and "Paper Birds" (retitled from "Pájaros en papel") from *Handmade* (retitled from *Hecho a Mano*) by Guadalupe Rodríguez. Copyright © 2009 by Guadalupe Rodríguez. Reprinted by permission of Editorial Amanuta Limitada and b small publishing.

Interrupting Chicken by David Ezra Stein. Copyright © 2010 by David Ezra Stein. Reprinted by permission of Candlewick Press, Somerville, MA, Editorial Juventud, and Recorded Books.

Sam & Dave Dig a Hole by Mac Barnett, illustrated by Jon Klassen. Text copyright © 2014 by Mac Barnett. Illustration copyright © 2014 by Jon Klassen. Reprinted by permission of Candlewick Press, Somerville, MA.

Credits